The First Family of
HOPE

The OBAMAS

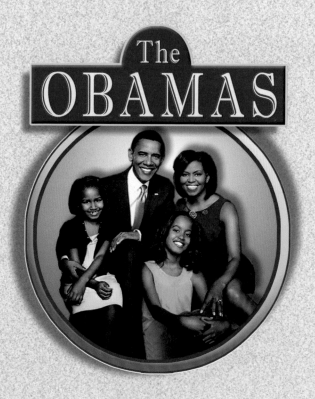

Barack

Michelle

Malia

Sasha

The Obama Family Tree

Obama Mania

Sasha

Gail Snyder

Mason Crest Publishers

Produced by 21st Century Publishing and Communications, Inc.

MASON CREST PUBLISHERS INC.
370 Reed Road
Broomall, Pennsylvania 19008
(866) MCP-BOOK (toll free)
www.masoncrest.com

Printed in the United States of America.

First Printing

9 8 7 6 5 4 3 2 1

Library of Congress Cataloging-in-Publication Data

Snyder, Gail.
    Sasha / Gail Snyder.
        p. cm. — (The Obamas : first family of hope)
    Includes bibliographical references and index.
    ISBN 978-1-4222-1480-0 (hardcover : alk. paper)
    ISBN 978-1-4222-1487-9 (pbk. : alk. paper)
    1. Obama, Sasha, 2001–   —Juvenile literature. 2. Obama, Sasha,
2001–   —Family—Juvenile literature. 3. Children of presidents—
United States—Biography—Juvenile literature. 4. Daughters—United
States—Biography—Juvenile literature. 5. Obama, Barack—Juvenile
literature. I. Title.
E909.O25S69 2009
973.932092—dc22
[B]   2009001466

Publisher's notes:
All quotations in this book come from original sources, and contain the spelling and grammatical inconsistencies of the original text.

The Web sites mentioned in this book were active at the time of publication. The publisher is not responsible for Web sites that have changed their addresses or discontinued operation since the date of publication. The publisher will review and update the Web site addresses each time the book is reprinted.

Contents

Introduction

On November 4, 2008, Barack Obama made history—he was the first black American to be elected president of the United States. The Obama family—Barack, wife Michelle, and daughters Malia and Sasha, became the first African-American first family.

THE FIRST FAMILY OF HOPE

The stories of the Obamas are fascinating and uniquely American. The six books in this series take you center stage and behind the scenes, with crafted and insightful storytelling, as well as hundreds of dynamic and telling photographs. Discover six unique inside perspectives on the Obama family's extraordinary journey and the Obama mania that surrounds it.

WHERE IT ALL BEGAN

Many generations ago, in the late 1600s, Barack's mother's ancestors arrived in colonial America as white emigrants from Europe, while his father's ancestors lived in villages in Kenya, Africa. Michelle's ancestors were shipped from Africa to America as slaves.

Generations later, Barack, son of a black father and a white mother, spent his childhood in Hawaii and Indonesia; while Michelle, a descendant of slaves, was growing up in Chicago. Later they both graduated from Harvard Law School, got married, and became proud parents of two beautiful daughters. Barack tackled injustice as a community organizer in Chicago, later entered politics, and was elected to the U.S. Senate.

"THE AUDACITY OF HOPE"

In 2004, at the Democratic National Convention, Barack Obama made an electrifying keynote speech, "The Audacity of Hope." He asked Americans to find unity in diversity and hope in the future. His message resonated with the attendees and millions of television viewers. Barack was catapulted from obscurity into the spotlight, and the Obama phenomenon had begun.

"YES WE CAN!"

On February 10, 2007, Barack announced his candidacy for the office of president of the United States. His family and legions of volunteers all over the country campaigned vigorously for him, and nearly two years later, the Obama family stood proudly in front of more than 240,000 supporters who gathered to hear Barack's victory speech. Tears streamed down the

The Obamas (left to right) Malia, Michelle, Sasha, and Barack, wave to their devoted fans. Barack has energized millions of people in the United States and around the world with his message of unity and hope.

faces of people who believed this was nothing short of a miracle. Tens of millions of television viewers worldwide watched and listened with a renewed sense of hope as President-elect Obama proclaimed:

> **❝This victory is yours. . . . If there is anyone out there who still doubts that America is a place where all things are possible; who still wonders if the dream of our founders is alive in our time; who still questions the power of our democracy, tonight is your answer.❞**

OBAMA FAMILY TIMELINE

1600s to 1700s
Barack Obama's mother's ancestors immigrate to the American colonies from Europe.

1936
Barack Obama, Sr., Barack's father, is born in a small village in Kenya, Africa.

1964
Barack's parents, Barack Obama, Sr. and Ann Dunham are divorced.

1700s to 1800s
Michelle Robinson Obama's ancestors arrive in the American colonies as slaves.

1937
Michelle's mother, Marian Shields, is born.

1967
Barack's mother marries Lolo Soetoro and moves the family to Soetoro's home country, Indonesia.

1850s
Michelle's great-great grandfather is born a slave in South Carolina.

1942
Barack's mother, Ann Dunham, is born in Kansas.

1971
Barack returns to Hawaii and lives with his grandparents.

1600　　1900　　1950　　1982

1912
Michelle's grandfather, Fraser Robinson Jr., is born.

1959
Barack Obama, Sr. comes to America as a student.

1979
Barack graduates from high school and enrolls in Occidental College in Los Angeles, California.

1918
Barack's grandfather, Stanley Dunham, is born.

February 21, 1961
Barack Obama, Sr. and Ann Dunham are married.

1922
Barack's grandmother, Madelyn Payne, is born.

August 4, 1961
Barack is born in Honolulu, Hawaii.

1981
Barack transfers to Columbia University in New York City.

1935
Michelle's father, Fraser Robinson III, is born.

January 17, 1964
Michelle is born in Chicago, Illinois.

1982
Barack's father dies in Kenya, Africa.

1988
Michelle graduates from Harvard Law School.

1995
Barack's first book, *Dreams from My Father*, is published.

November 2, 2008
Barack's grandmother dies in Hawaii.

1988
Barack enters Harvard Law School.

1998
Barack and Michelle's first daughter, Malia, is born.

November 4, 2008
Barack is elected the first African-American president of the United States.

1990
Barack is elected president of the *Harvard Law Review*.

2001
Barack and Michelle's second daughter, Sasha, is born.

January 20, 2009
Barack is sworn in as the 44th president of the United States.

1991
Barack graduates from Harvard Law School.

July 2004
Barack delivers keynote speech at Democratic National Convention.

1983   1995   2006   2009

1988
Barack visits his relatives in Kenya, Africa.

1996
Barack is elected to the Illinois State Senate.

August 2008
Barack is nominated as the Democratic candidate for the presidency.

1985
Michelle graduates from Princeton University.

1995
Barack's mother dies.

February 10, 2007
Barack announces his candidacy for the office of president of the United States of America.

1985
Barack moves to Chicago, Illinois, to work as a community organizer.

1992
Barack and Michelle are married.

2006
Barack's second book, *The Audacity of Hope*, is published.

1983
Barack graduates from Columbia University.

1992
Barack begins teaching at the University of Chicago Law School.

November 2004
Barack is elected to the U.S. Senate.

Sasha with her daddy, President-elect Barack Obama, after his acceptance speech at Grant Park, Chicago, November 4, 2008. Winning the election meant the Obamas would soon move to the White House, and Sasha's dream of getting a new puppy would come true.

1

Proud First Daughter

For seven-year-old Natasha Obama, who is usually called Sasha, the two years her father spent campaigning for the presidency of the United States were no big deal. Full of energy and unable to sit still for long periods of time, Sasha didn't quite understand why crowds of people gave her father props for every word he said.

When she was on the campaign trail she walked away from his speeches whenever she could. To her his words were little more than "blah, blah, blah," and Barack Obama was just the daddy who came home from campaign trips and thoughtlessly left his suitcase on top of her shoes in the mudroom of the family's Hyde Park home in Chicago.

ELECTION DAY

But on November 4, 2008, even Sasha knew something special was going on and that her father was at the center of it.

The day began as most weekdays did for Sasha. She had to get up, eat breakfast, and be ready for school, even though this was the day people around the world had waited for: the day her father had the opportunity to be elected the first African-American president of the United States.

Before Sasha could go to school, though, she first went to the nearby polling place to watch her parents vote. The family drove to Shoesmith Elementary School, and their arrival at the polling place caused a buzz of excitement in the large orderly crowd already waiting in a long line to vote that morning. Swelling the numbers even more were television and newspaper reporters covering the story of the presidential nominee and his wife voting with their kids in tow. The crowd parted enough to allow Sasha and her parents to go right in to vote, which they did by standing in adjacent voting booths. Sasha's mom, Michelle, took longer to vote

Hyde Park Celebrates

Sasha, her older sister Malia, and their family are well known in Hyde Park, a racially diverse community near the University of Chicago where her mother used to work and Sasha went to school. On election day, the residents of Hyde Park were especially proud of the Obamas.

Among the celebrants were people who knew Barack from the Hyde Park Hair Salon, the place where Barack faithfully got his hair trimmed until the Secret Service told him he could no longer go there because its big plate glass window made it a security risk.

But that didn't matter to the crowd gathered at the salon on election night, who exuberantly exclaimed, "Yes we did! Yes we did!" when Barack Obama won.

Meanwhile, at a nearby restaurant other people had gathered to experience the election results in Obama's 'hood. Said restaurant customer Paula Dixon, "This is Obama's stomping grounds; what better place to be?"

Children in Hyde Park, Chicago, rally on election day to urge voters to vote for Barack Obama. Everyone in Hyde Park was proud of Barack, and customers in restaurants, hair salons, and stores all wished him well because he was their neighbor as well as their candidate.

than Barack and he joked that he was a little worried about whom she was voting for.

DADDY'S BIG DEAL

There can be no doubt that Barack was stoked as he chose himself on the presidential ballot. But he mentioned another high to the press. He said,

❝ **The journey ends, but voting with my daughters, that was a big deal.** ❞

Sasha (right) and her sister Malia watch their dad, Barack Obama, cast his ballot at Shoesmith Elementary School, Chicago, November 4, 2008. Barack said it was very important to him to have his daughters with him when he voted, at the end of his long campaign.

They left the polling place and Michelle took Sasha to University of Chicago Lab School, where Sasha attended second grade. Sasha was not allowed to miss a single day of school throughout her father's nearly two-year campaign for the presidency. Her parents were not going to let election day be any different. Besides, Sasha would soon need to say goodbye to her classmates at Chicago Lab if her dad won the presidency.

Sasha's New School

When Sasha and her family moved into the White House, she said goodbye to her old school and friends. The Obama girls now attend Sidwell Friends School, the same school attended by Chelsea Clinton, daughter of former President Bill Clinton and Secretary of State Hillary Clinton, and Tricia and Julie Nixon, daughters of former president Richard Nixon.

Sasha goes to the school's campus in Bethesda, Maryland, where she will stay until she reaches fifth grade. She is no longer in the same building as Malia, who attends Sidwell's campus in Northwest Washington, which houses students through high school.

One of the reasons Sasha's parents chose Sidwell was that the Secret Service, the federal agency charged with protecting the first family, thought it would be a safe place for her to get an excellent education. Sasha even has her own code name given to her by the Secret Service: Rosebud.

At the same time Sasha was going through her normal school day, her parents were also taking care of business. Barack campaigned in Indiana, sat for interviews with reporters, and managed to find a couple of hours to play basketball with some friends, an election day tradition that helps him chill. Michelle also did her share of television interviews until it was time to pick up Sasha at school.

GETTING READY

After school Sasha and her sister were whisked off to get their hair done. Then it was time to go home again where Barack hung out with Sasha and Malia, enjoying a leisurely steak dinner with the family. They talked about the election results, which were starting to come in and showing unmistakable signs of a big win for Barack over Republican candidate John McCain.

At 10 P.M. the family left for the hotel suite their friends and family members were already occupying to wait out the official word that Barack had been elected 44th president of the United States. As that official word was announced by CNN, the family took the news calmly. Sasha's grandmother, Marian Robinson, recalled,

❝ Everybody was quiet. I can't tell you how subdued it was. We weren't like the people in the stands—you know, yelling and screaming. ❞

GRANT PARK

A short while later Sasha and her family took a **motorcade** ride to nearby Grant Park, where 240,000 Obama supporters were standing shoulder to shoulder waiting for the soon-to-be first family to make its appearance. The orderly crowd sang the "Star-Spangled Banner," cheered, cried, waved Obama signs and Obama dolls, and celebrated the first African-American president's victory.

Sasha, her family, and hundreds of their friends waited in a tent for the moment Barack would make his acceptance speech. One of Sasha's friends, who is her age, exclaimed, "Mommy, are all these people here to see Uncle Barack?"

Indeed they were. Finally an announcer's voice boomed over the loudspeaker: "Ladies and gentlemen, the next first family of the United States of America!" The family held hands and walked out on the stage to thunderous applause. Barack then addressed the crowd, first thanking some of the people who helped him win the election. Some of those words were reserved for Sasha. Said Barack,

President-elect Barack Obama talks to Sasha on stage, next to his wife, Michelle, and daughter Malia, at his election night rally in Grant Park, Chicago. Over 200,000 people celebrated the election of America's first African-American president, cheering and chanting his campaign slogan, "Yes We Can!"

    ❝ Sasha and Malia, I love you so much. You have earned the new puppy that will be coming to the White House with us. ❞

Up long past her usual 8:30 bedtime, no one could have blamed Sasha if she thought she was dreaming as she heard the news about the puppy and later, when her father was done speaking, when he held her high in his arms, every bit as much the first daddy as he was "Mr. President."

Barack as a boy with his grandfather Stanley Dunham at the beach in Hawaii, 1963. Growing up as a child of mixed races wasn't easy during a time of prejudice, but Barack is proud of his multicultural, multi-ethnic heritage.

② Mixed Race Family

Like his daughter, Sasha, Barack is a dog lover with a special fondness for canines that don't have a **pedigree**. Barack identifies with mutts because he sees himself as one. He and Sasha are a mixture of different cultures and ethnicities, and can count among their relatives people who live on three continents.

Barack's mother, Stanley Ann Dunham, was a white woman from Kansas who fell in love with a black man from Kenya, Barack Obama Sr. They met while both were studying at the University of Hawaii. Stanley Ann was only 18 years old when her son, Barack Hussein Obama Jr., was born.

ABSENTEE FATHER

The marriage lasted three years before ending in divorce after Barack's father left Hawaii to study in Massachusetts and then returned to Kenya to live. He had hardly any contact at all with Barack, who recalls,

❝ He and my mother divorced when I was only two years old, and for most of my life I knew him only through the letters he sent and the stories my mother and grandparents told. ❞

Laws That Kept Races Apart

Madelyn Dunham, Barack's grandmother, was not happy when her daughter Stanley Ann told her she wanted to marry a black man from Kenya. In 1961, marriages between black and white people were uncommon, and some states had laws against the practice. These anti-miscegenation laws were still in effect six years later when the U.S. Supreme Court ruled a Virginia anti-miscegenation law was unconstitutional. In 2000, the U.S. Census Bureau reported that some 7 million Americans, or about 2.4 percent of the population, designated themselves as multiracial.

Among the famous Americans who have been born into multiracial homes are baseball star Derek Jeter, reporter Soledad O'Brien, professional golfer Tiger Woods, pop singer Mariah Carey, model Tyson Beckford, actresses Halle Berry, Jennifer Beals, Rosario Dawson, Jessica Alba, and Tina and Tamara Mowry, and actors Vin Diesel and Dwayne Johnson, formerly known as the professional wrestler, The Rock.

In many respects, Stanley Ann and Barack Obama Sr. came from two different worlds. When they met, Stanley Ann was a college freshman, a self-confident only child who did not want to lead an ordinary life. Barack Obama Sr. had completed his undergraduate education and was in graduate school—and he already had

Barack's parents, Barack Obama Sr. and Ann Dunham, during Obama Sr.'s brief visit to the United States in 1971. Never really knowing his father affected Barack deeply, and when Sasha and Malia were born, he vowed to be a devoted father to his daughters.

two children from his first marriage to a Kenyan woman. What the couple had in common was a love of politics and a need to debate important topics, she in a passionate but quiet way, and he in a louder more assertive manner that earned him more attention.

EXTENDED FAMILY

Only two years after her marriage to Barack Sr. broke up, Stanley Ann remarried, this time to an Indonesian man with whom she had a daughter named Maya. Barack and Maya grew up together and have been very close ever since. The family lived for a time in Indonesia before returning to Hawaii when the marriage ended.

Barack Sr. also went on to multiple marriages, fathering eight children who are Sasha's step-aunts and step-uncles, before his death in an automobile accident in 1982.

One of those step-aunts is a woman named Auma Obama, who lives in Kenya and describes her own unusual family background this way:

> **❝ My daughter's father is British. My Mom's brother is married to a Russian. I have a brother in China engaged to a Chinese woman. ❞**

GREAT-GRANDMOTHER TOOT

When Barack was in high school, Stanley Ann returned to Indonesia to work and at his insistence, Barack remained in Hawaii with his grandparents, Madelyn and Stanley Dunham.

Barack was tight with his grandparents, particularly with Madelyn, whom he called Toot. Barack's name for his grandmother stems from the Hawaiian word for grandparent, which is "tutu." This relationship lasted until Toot died, just two days before Barack was elected president. Even though she was in ill health, Toot had been able to follow the election campaign. She understood that her grandson was poised to topple the racial barrier that had kept an African American from attaining the highest office in America. Sasha got to know Toot well because the family often vacationed in Hawaii to spend time with her. Sasha did not get to know her grandmother Stanley Ann, who died in 1995, six years before Sasha was born.

THE ROBINSONS

Barack met Sasha's mother, Michelle Robinson, when they both worked at the same law firm and Michelle was given the job of familiarizing Barack with the firm. Michelle at first resisted Barack's attempts to ask her out but eventually relented. Barack noticed right away that Michelle's family was quite a bit different from his own. Michelle's parents had a long and successful marriage and had

Barack and his grandparents at his high school graduation in Hawaii, 1979. The Dunhams' constant emotional support was a big influence on Barack. He was glad Sasha and her sister got to know their great-grandmother, "Toot," on many family visits to Hawaii.

stayed in Chicago the whole time. What is more, although both of Michelle's parents worked, they made it a priority to focus on the needs of Michelle and her older brother, Craig, who is now a college basketball coach.

Michelle could also trace her family's roots in the United States back to the 19th century when her great-great grandfather, Jim Robinson, was a slave on a South Carolina plantation. Her family also believes that one of their ancestors owned slaves. She says,

❝ Somewhere there was a slave owner—or a white family in my great-grandfather's time that gave him a place, a home that helped him build a life—that again led to me. So who were these people? I would argue they're just as much a part of my history as my great-grandfather. ❞

Although Michelle's and Barack's families had their differences, Michelle also thought they had enough in common on which to build a strong foundation. She saw parallels between Barack's hardworking grandparents and her own parents, and even with Stanley Ann who did her best to raise Barack as a single mother.

Sasha's parents wed in 1992 and consciously decided to model their roles as parents on the Robinson family. Indeed, Barack and

A wedding photo of Barack and Michelle with Michelle's mother Marian Robinson and Barack's mother Ann, 1992. Ann died before Sasha was born, but Sasha is very close to Marian, who moved into the White House with the first family to help take care of her grandchildren.

Michelle have said that the run for the presidency would never have been possible without the help of Michelle's mother, Marian Robinson, who watched Sasha and her sister when their parents could not do so because of the demands of campaigning. Marian remains devoted to Sasha and moved to Washington to be closer to her grandchild, leaving behind a comfortable life in Chicago.

No Birthday Presents

Sasha's grandmother Marian Robinson has had a very big impact on her life—including the way she celebrates her birthday. Sasha usually can invite lots of friends to a party and eat birthday cake, but she never gets a birthday present from her mom and dad. The Obamas don't want Sasha to grow up spoiled, and years ago Robinson convinced them that downplaying the children's birthdays was for their own good.

Sasha gets to choose what she and her friends will do on her birthday, which falls on June 10. Some of Sasha's favorite activities are playing tennis and piano, watching the television show *Hannah Montana*, gymnastics, singing, and dancing. She is a major fan of the Jonas Brothers. Her favorite foods are macaroni and cheese and fried chicken, but they are occasional treats. Sasha's parents prefer that she eats healthy foods.

A STABLE FAMILY LIFE

Barack's most devoted sibling is his half-sister Maya Soetoro-Ng, who shared the same mother and regards him as a father figure. Maya knows the importance her brother places on having an ordinary life for his own daughters, even in the midst of extraordinary events like running for the presidency or living in the White House. She said,

> **Our childhood was constant moving and adventure but little stability. Barack wants for his girls a rootedness and community that he didn't have.**

Sasha plays on a swing in a park. A lively and outgoing child, Sasha is now used to her family being in the spotlight. She always smiles and waves to the cameras when she is out in public with her parents.

3

The Ham

Sasha was born on June 10, 2001, in Chicago. She was, as her dad would recall, as "calm and as beautiful as Malia" at birth. As Sasha grew she has developed an outgoing personality, and is comfortable being the center of attention. Sasha likes to be the life of the party.

She is also used to being taken care of by babysitters and her grandmother Marian, who often watched the girls when Michelle could not.

At the time she was born her father had been in the Illinois Senate for two terms. By her second birthday he had announced a run for the U.S. Senate, which proved successful.

Barack's frequent absences from Sasha's life have always seemed normal to her, although she loves to cuddle with her dad when he is around. Spending time with his daughters has always been a priority for Barack.

MAKING LASTING MEMORIES

Mindful that Michelle has been a more hands-on parent than he has, Barack volunteered to plan Sasha's fifth birthday party. Such an assignment would be a challenge for most fathers, and knowing that Michelle likes every detail to be perfect made Barack even more determined not to mess up. The party was at a gymnastics studio and was to feature pizza, birthday cake, and juice boxes. The day of the party Barack was nervous as he waited for the pizza deliveryman. A late pizza delivery was the only glitch and Michelle

Sasha gets a kiss from her father, Barack Obama, at his Senate office. When her dad is around, Sasha loves to cuddle with him. To Barack, spending time with his daughters is very special. He even organized Sasha's fifth birthday party all by himself.

was pleased. Barack described what happened next in his book, *The Audacity of Hope*:

> **❝As a grand finale, after all the pizza was eaten and the juice boxes drunk, after we had sung 'Happy Birthday' and eaten some cake, the gymnastics instructor gathered all the kids around an old, multicolored parachute and told Sasha to sit at its center. On the count of three, Sasha was hoisted up into the air and back down again, then up for a second time, and then for a third. And each time she rose above the billowing sail, she laughed and laughed with a look of pure joy.**
>
> **I wonder if Sasha will remember that moment when she is grown. Probably not; it seems as if I can retrieve only the barest fragments of memory from when I was five. But I suspect that the happiness she felt on that parachute registers permanently in her; that such moments accumulate and embed themselves in a child's character, becoming a part of their soul.❞**

Sasha's Cool Dad

Barack once told a reporter, "I think I'm a pretty cool dad." Some reasons Sasha's dad is cool are: he listens when she tells him what is cool and what isn't for adult behavior; he called home every night while he was on the campaign trail, and hooked a Web camera to his computer so he could see Sasha and Malia; and he tries his best to get to as many soccer games and dance recitals as possible and feels bad when he misses them. During the presidential campaign, Barack came home to take Sasha trick-or-treating in their Chicago neighborhood.

Barack also has more than a half-million friends on his MySpace page and is the king of text messaging. In fact, he texted the name of his vice presidential selection to 2.9 million people from his own cell phone. With his texting bill reaching $290,000 for that call alone, Barack won't be able to tell Sasha to put a lid on it when she texts her friends

There were other good times, too. Every time Barack got elected he shared a celebration—and the limelight—with his daughter and family. Even when the family took trips to the Chicago Zoo, Sasha might find that strangers would come up to her family and ask her questions, lured by the chance to spend time with her well-known and influential father.

A MEMORABLE SPEECH

As it turned out, Sasha's father became even more well known outside Chicago in 2004 when he was asked to give the **keynote address** at the Democratic National Convention in Boston. The speech he gave that July night made him instantly known around the country as an up-and-coming young politician with possible presidential ambitions.

He set the tone of the speech with these words:

> **❝I stand here today, grateful for the diversity of my heritage, aware that my parents' dreams live on in my two precious daughters. I stand here knowing that my story is part of the larger American story, that I owe a debt to all of those who came before me, and that, in no other country on earth, is my story even possible.❞**

Both Barack and Michelle had been nervous about how Barack's speech would be received. Michelle told Barack before he went on stage, "Just don't screw it up, buddy."

A DAZZLING SMILE

Four months after that speech Barack was elected to the U.S. Senate, receiving an awesome 70 percent of the vote. Once again, Barack included Sasha in his victory celebration, taking her along to his swearing-in ceremony at which the vice president of the United States administered the oath of office. In a photograph taken that day, Malia looks shyly at the camera but Sasha flashes a dazzling smile.

Issue 719
November 24, 2008

US WEEKLY

TWILIGHT!
Meet the
Hot Stars

Obama with
Malia (left)
and Sasha

BARACK OBAMA'S GIRLS

'I Think I'm a Pretty Cool Dad'

- Barack & Michelle's plan to keep their family life normal

Sasha with her dad and sister Malia on the cover of *People* magazine. Barack thinks he is a pretty cool dad; he always tries to attend as many of Sasha's activities as possible and listens to his daughters' opinions on what is cool and not cool for adults to do.

Barack recalls the scene in his book, *The Audacity of Hope*:

" In the Old Senate Chamber, I joined my wife, Michelle, and our two daughters for a reenactment of the ceremony and picture-taking with Vice President Cheney (true to form, then six-year-old Malia demurely shook the vice president's hand, while then three-year-old Sasha decided instead to slap palms with the man before twirling around to wave for the cameras). "

Barack Obama re-enacts being sworn in as a senator by Vice President Dick Cheney, January 4, 2005. Michelle, Malia, and Sasha are at his side. Sasha was only three years old, but she slapped hands with the vice president and then smiled for the cameras.

VISITING THE WHITE HOUSE

Sasha also got to visit the White House for the first time that year. Too young to really grasp its historical significance, the highlight of her visit was petting President Bush's black Scottish terrier, Barney.

Unusual White House Happenings

Kids sometimes do funny things—even if they happen to be the children of presidents. For example, Tad Lincoln, son of Abraham Lincoln, once startled his mother and her visitors by bringing his herd of goats into the White House. Amy Carter, daughter of President Jimmy Carter, who was just two years older than Sasha when she came to the White House, had permission to roller skate inside the family's living quarters.

Caroline Kennedy, daughter of President John F. Kennedy, was allowed to ride her pony Macaroni on the White House grounds. President Theodore Roosevelt's son Quentin sneaked his pony Algonquin into the White House to entertain his brother.

And, in what may have been the wildest time of all, Susan Ford, daughter of President Gerald Ford, brought her entire high school class to the White House for their senior prom.

Sasha and her sister next visited the White House four years later, after her dad had won the presidential election. This time Sasha realized that she was visiting her soon-to-be new home. Serving as her tour guides were President Bush's twin daughters, Barbara and Jenna, who are in their mid-twenties. The Bush twins showed Sasha all the secret places only a kid in the White House would know about. They also encouraged Sasha to take a running leap onto a high White House bed, which left them all giggling.

Barack Obamas relaxes with Sasha. A letter to his daughters explained why Barack ran for president: "[T]he greatest joy in my life was the joy I saw in yours. . . . my own life wouldn't count for much unless I was able to ensure that you had every opportunity for happiness and fulfillment in yours. . . . that's why I ran for President."

Daddy Runs for President

Call it a bribe, a reward, or an incentive, but Sasha and Malia insisted that their father give them something in exchange for letting him run for president. Win or lose, the children proposed that Barack and Michelle promise them a puppy, preferably a fluffy white one they could call Snowball.

FAMILY DISCUSSIONS

Barack and Michelle agreed that the girls could have their puppy when the presidential campaign was over. But they also took great pains to explain to Sasha and Malia how things might change for the family during Barack's historic run for the presidency. They had these discussions at the dinner table and in the mornings when the entire family would snuggle and talk in Michelle and Barack's bed.

Involving Sasha in his decision-making was important to Barack not only because the presidential race would potentially alter their lives for good, but also because Barack had long maintained that public service is something he had undertaken to make the world a better place for his daughters and other children of their generation. Once when he was asked what inspired him most Barack said,

> **" I'm inspired by the love people have for their children. And I'm inspired by my own children, how full they make my heart. They make me want to work to make the world a little bit better. And they make me want to be a better man. "**

What Kids Say About Barack

Even though they can't vote yet, school-age children can write letters. Children at an elementary and a middle school in Bridgeport, Connecticut, were asked to write letters to Barack Obama after he won the presidential election.

One middle school girl wrote,

> "Having an African-American president in the White House is such a joy. . . . I jumped with joy, screamed and danced."

Another middle school girl said,

> "You are a huge role model to all minority children. Many minority children probably thought that they can't be successful people. You made a personal change to me because it opened my eyes."

A 14-year-old's letter read,

> "You becoming president is an important part of my life. You becoming president saved a whole bunch of kids, including myself, because I was on the verge of just giving up and just doing bad in school. . . . Now I know that dreams do come true."

The Obamas pose for a family photo. Barack has said he is inspired by parents' love for their children. His love for his own children has made him want to work hard to make the world a better place for them.

Barack and Michelle pledged to keep Sasha's life as normal as possible even as her father's life would dramatically change. She would continue to go to school, have play dates, take piano and dance lessons, and do all of her usual stuff with her mother or grandmother Marian, who was always on hand to provide emotional support.

A FORMAL ANNOUNCEMENT

Only then did Barack take the next step, which was to make a formal announcement on February 10, 2007, on the steps of the Old State Capitol Building in Springfield, Illinois. When he did so his family was by his side, with Sasha dressed in a boldly patterned black and white coat accented by a rose colored ski cap, scarf, and gloves.

Barack chose the location for its symbolism. It was the same place where Abraham Lincoln had launched his presidential campaign. Barack greatly admired President Lincoln for his willingness to work with those who opposed him and for

Barack , Michelle, Sasha, and Malia wave to supporters after Barack announced his presidential candidacy on February 10, 2007. Barack chose the Old State Capitol in Springfield, Illinois, for the event because Abraham Lincoln had begun his presidential campaign there in 1860.

his eloquent yet plain-spoken language to Americans caught in the grip of the Civil War.

Addressing supporters who came out that cold, windy day in February Barack said,

❝ It's humbling, but in my heart I know you didn't come here just for me, you came here because you believe in what this country can be. In the face of war, you believe there can be peace. In the face of despair, you believe there can be hope. In the face of politics that's shut you out, that's told you to settle, that's divided us for too long, you believe we can be one people, reaching for what's possible, building the more perfect union. ❞

African-American Candidates

Barack Obama was not the first African American to campaign for the presidency. His election to the nation's top office owes a debt to other African Americans who came before him. Each one who tried made it easier for the next candidate to break down voters' prejudices.

First to try was Democrat Shirley Chisholm, a U.S. congresswoman who in 1972 ran a brief campaign that opened the door just a crack. In 1984, the Reverend Jesse Jackson, a civil rights leader, won 3.5 million votes in his campaign for the presidency. Four years later, Jackson tried once more, this time picking up 6.9 million votes, good enough to earn him second place after Michael Dukakis, who went on to lose the presidential race to Republican George H. W. Bush. In 2004, two African Americans participated in the Democratic primaries—Illinois Senator Carol Moseley Braun and New York City minister and activist Al Sharpton.

On the Republican side, Alan Keyes, a former U.S. representative to the United Nations, ran twice, once in 1996 and once in 2000. There has also been one African-American third party candidate for president, Leonora Fulani, a New York psychologist who vied for the presidency in 1988.

Hillary Clinton and John Edwards, two other candidates, had already announced their own presidential campaigns for the Democratic nomination. Clinton was a second-term senator from New York and had been first lady for eight years. Edwards, a former senator from North Carolina, had been a vice presidential candidate in 2004. The Democratic primary race would also soon be joined by other candidates as well.

CAMPAIGNING AROUND THE COUNTRY

Following his announcement, Barack began a near-constant round of campaigning across the country that took him away from Sasha even more than usual. Calls home every night from the candidate on the road were a poor substitute for having daddy at home, of course, and in the summer Sasha and her sister and mother joined Barack in a rented RV so he didn't have to choose between campaigning and being with his kids.

Barack's overriding theme to his primary race was one of change. He framed his lack of experience in Washington, D.C., as a positive trait that would help him shake things up. He also pointed out that he was one of the first and most consistent opponents of the war in Iraq, which Clinton had supported and the American people had come to oppose.

THE REVEREND JEREMIAH WRIGHT

If there was a rough patch in Barack's well-run campaign, it was in his initial support for his pastor and friend, the Reverend Jeremiah Wright, of Chicago's Trinity United Church of Christ. During the two decades that Barack belonged to the church, the Reverend Wright had married Barack and Michelle and baptized both Sasha and Malia. He had even provided the inspiration for the title of Barack's bestselling book, *The Audacity of Hope*.

But some of Wright's sermons were highly controversial. Bits and pieces of them were being aired on cable news shows and YouTube, earning them a much wider audience than the one in his pews on Sunday mornings. In addition to introducing the world

Sasha enjoys a bumper car ride with her father at the Iowa State Fair in Des Moines, Iowa, in August 2007. That summer the whole family went on the campaign trail in a rented RV so that Barack could spend more time with Sasha and Malia.

to his radical views, Wright's comments also injected the concept of racism into the presidential campaign, which Barack did not want to do.

After a series of disputes over the controversial remarks by the Reverend Wright, Barack had no choice but to distance himself from his pastor. Finally in May, 2008 he resigned as a member of Trinity United Church of Christ.

A FATHER'S DAY MESSAGE

On Father's Day, June 15, 2008, when Barack was ready to give a speech about fatherhood, he did not take his message to Wright's church, as he would have in the past. Instead, he chose the Apostolic Church of God, another black church on the South Side of Chicago.

Sasha sat in the front pew with her sister Malia and mother, listening as her father spoke about parenting and personal responsibilities to a packed audience, saying,

> **I know the toll it took on me, not having a father in the house. . . . The hole in your heart when you don't have a male figure in the home who can guide you and lead you. So I resolved many years ago that it was my obligation to break the cycle—that if I could be anything in life, I would be a good father to my girls; that if I could give them anything, I would give them that rock—that foundation—on which to build their lives. And that would be the greatest gift I could offer.**

Sasha Immortalized in Painting

Sasha's appearance at the 2008 Democratic National Convention in Denver will long be remembered through photographs made at the event and at least one oil painting. Artist Elizabeth Peyton, working from a photograph, painted Michelle as she listened to Barack accept his party's nomination at the convention, with a sleepy Sasha curled up in her lap.

Peyton's painting of Michelle and Sasha was exhibited at the New Museum in New York along with other works from the artist. Peyton is known for her portraits of famous people. The painting also appeared in a magazine spread and traveled to Minneapolis, London, and the Netherlands before being purchased by a private collector.

Once in office, it is common to have the president and first lady sit for portraits. But the Obama family was ahead of the game with a family portrait before they even settled in the White House.

Barack Obama speaks at Apostolic Church of God in Chicago, June 15, 2008, while daughters Sasha and Malia, and wife Michelle look on. On that particular Father's Day, Barack spoke about the urgency and importance of fathers providing a strong and solid foundation for their children. Barack's image as a family man found favor with many voters.

Sasha yawns during Barack's speech at Invesco Field at the Democratic National Convention in Denver, August 28, 2008. This mother and daughter moment was captured by artist Elizabeth Peyton in a painting that later appeared in a New York museum and traveled the country and the world.

SECURING THE DEMOCRATIC NOMINATION

Barack got off to a very strong start in the primary season's first contest, the Iowa **caucuses**. He came in first; Edwards finished second; and Clinton, regarded then as the front-runner, came in third. However, five days later, Senator Clinton defeated Obama in the New Hampshire primary.

On Super Tuesday, when 25 states held their primaries and caucuses, Barack emerged victorious in 13 of those contests. Like a boulder rolling down a great hillside, the Obama campaign gained a lot more momentum after Barack won the next 11 contests in a row, which earned him many important delegates committed to supporting him at the Democratic National Convention that summer.

Nearly two years after Barack announced he would run for president of the United States, he earned enough delegates to be declared the Democratic nominee. Barack had convincingly beaten Clinton, raised significantly more in campaign contributions, and fielded a more diverse coalition of volunteers.

Barack had also been right when he judged that voters were more attracted to change and the new political direction he promised than to Clinton's call for an experienced stateswoman at the helm.

Next stop was the general election pitting Barack against Republic nominee Senator John McCain, a decorated Vietnam War hero who is decades older.

Sasha, Michelle, and Malia speak to Barack via satellite at the 2008 Democratic National Convention. Barack's nomination there led to his election as president and the family's move to Washington, where Sasha became the youngest child to live in the White House since the 1960s.

Youngest Kid in the White House

If someone wants to know what the real Barack Obama is like, they have only to ask Sasha. In a rare interview in 2008, when her father was running for president, Sasha got the chance to talk about her famous daddy on *Access Hollywood*. It was the only television show interview Barack and Michelle let Sasha do.

Even then they regretted the decision because they wanted to keep their kids' lives as normal as possible.

Barack commented to *Access*'s reporter that his children "basically cut out when I start talking." During the interview a bored Sasha asked if they would soon be getting ice cream—an activity she clearly preferred to sitting down and talking with adults even if a camera crew was present. Then she let slip an intimate detail about her father. She said,

❝Everybody should like ice cream, except Daddy. My dad doesn't like sweets.❞

Later in the interview Sasha became more animated when asked by the reporter if she would like moving into the White House. She replied, "It would be very cool."

Of course Barack and Michelle had tried to do fun things with their kids when they came along on the campaign trail. Typically, they let the kids shoot water pistols, play the card game Uno, visit zoos and museums, and do other things that had nothing to do with selling the public on dad's ideas for change in government. And Barack would read to Sasha when she asked him, even if his voice was about to give out because of all the talking he was required to do in the campaign.

Is There a First Cookie?

While their daddy was campaigning in Iowa, Sasha and Malia were with him and craving cookies. They had previously been to a small diner in town and fell in love with some chocolate chunk cookies they wanted to have again. Somehow the girls' love for the cookies became a news story that ran in newspapers across the country.

As a result, the Baby Boomers Café in Des Moines went from selling several hundred cookies a week to selling thousands of the treats each day. Because of the Sasha and Malia connection, the café's owners were able to hire more people to turn out more cookies, even shipping them all over the country. Café co-owner Rodney Maxfield said,

"We're known as the cookie guys now and everybody wants to come in. We're the hot destination spot in Iowa now and everybody wants pictures of us and autographs and pictures of us with the cookies."

TEASING BARACK AT THE CONVENTION

Sasha also spent some time with Michelle, who addressed the Democratic National Convention in Denver in August. While her mother was doing a run-through of her speech, Sasha grabbed the **gavel** on the convention stage. Sasha held it triumphantly in the air before smacking it on the lectern as a big smile played across her face.

Later that night when Michelle finished her speech before the delegates, she told Sasha and her sister that she had a surprise for them. Both girls were disappointed that the surprise was only a satellite link with their dad. They were hoping that it was a performance by the Jonas Brothers, their favorite musicians.

a) Sasha looks up at her mother as Craig Robinson, Michelle's brother, looks on before the opening of the Democratic National Convention in Denver in August, 2008. b) While her mother rehearses her speech, Sasha happily bangs the gavel that would later open the convention.

But when Barack's image was projected that night in Denver, Sasha, who was paying strict attention to what he was saying, quickly caught him in a goof. When Barack absentmindedly said he was calling from both Kansas City and St. Louis, Sasha called him out on it. "Daddy, what city are you in?" she teased.

DELEGATE SERVICE DAY

On August 27, the third day of the convention, Sasha joined Malia and their mother in assembling care packages for troops serving in Iraq and Afghanistan. Michelle was the co-chair of the Democratic National Convention's Delegate Service Day. That

Sasha, Malia, and Michelle help assemble care packages for troops overseas during the Democratic National Convention's Delegate Service Day, August 27, 2008. Sasha enjoyed this part of the campaign because she likes helping other people.

was the day delegates were asked to participate in service-oriented projects that included canned food sorting, painting at local schools, serving meals at shelters, tree planting, and park maintenance. The projects were organized at various sites throughout the Denver area, allowing delegates to contribute to the people and organizations that hosted the Democratic National Convention.

A NOMINATION AND A PROMISE

Also on August 27, Barack officially received his party's nomination for President. On August 28, Barack accepted the nomination at an outdoor rally held at Invesco Field, home of the Denver Broncos football team. Once again, Sasha and her family were at his side, this time as a crowd of 84,000 people listened to her father address them from a stage that made him look presidential. Surrounded by 24 American flags waving in the breeze and the constant flashes of cameras recording the moment, Barack said,

> **"This country of ours has more wealth than any other nation, but that's not what makes us rich. We have the most powerful military on Earth, but that's not what makes us strong. Our universities and our culture are the envy of the world, but that's not what keeps the world coming to our shores.**
>
> **Instead, it is that American spirit—that American promise—that pushes us forward even when the path is uncertain; that binds us together in spite of our differences; that makes us fix our eye not on what is seen, but what is unseen; that better place around the bend. That promise is our greatest inheritance. It's a promise I make to my daughters when I tuck them in at night, and a promise that you make to yours—a promise that has led immigrants to cross oceans and pioneers to travel west; a promise that led workers to picket lines, and women to reach for the ballot."**

THE GENERAL ELECTION

Once the convention was over the Obama presidential campaign had eight weeks until the country would elect its leader. Barack and his vice presidential running mate, Senator Joe Biden, faced off against Republican presidential nominee Senator John McCain, a Vietnam war hero, and his running mate Sarah Palin, the young governor of Alaska.

Sasha and Barack greet Bruce Springsteen during a rally in Cleveland, Ohio in November 2008. The campaign seemed great fun when Sasha got to meet some of the famous people who supported Barack. This excitement continued into the inauguration celebrations, when Sasha met Miley Cyrus and the Jonas Brothers.

McCain and Palin were having difficulties finding sympathetic voters because of a slowdown in the U.S. economy, their support of the unpopular war in Iraq, and their loyalty to President Bush, whose public approval levels were extremely low.

Meanwhile Democrats were experiencing a surge of interest from young and first-time voters and **independents** who were ready to put the contentious years of the Bush administration behind them.

On November 4, 2008, the day the Obama family voted at Shoesmith Elementary School in Chicago, Barack captured 53 percent of the vote and became the first African American elected president of the United States. That meant the Obamas were moving to the White House.

AFTER THE ELECTION

After the election Barack returned home to Chicago to spend some time with his wife and children. Before Thanksgiving the family worked at a food bank in Chicago, handing out the fixings for a turkey dinner to needy families who waited in line in the cold to receive them. Barack and Michelle wanted Sasha and Malia to see for themselves that some people living in Chicago's South Side were not as privileged as they are and that the girls had an obligation to help those in need. The family also took a two-week Hawaiian vacation shortly before the inauguration. They then moved to Washington, D.C., in time for Sasha to start school at Sidwell Friends after the holiday break.

Sasha moved into the White House on January 20, 2008, the same day that George and Laura Bush moved out, in a smoothly orchestrated performance that occurs each time there is a change in presidential families. The move-in was part of an all-day celebration that began in the morning with Sasha's father taking the oath of office by placing his hand on the same Bible used by Abraham Lincoln when he was sworn in. Sasha had a first-class view of the proceedings, surrounded not only by her own family but also by Supreme Court justices, former presidents, and congressmen.

YOUNG CHILDREN IN THE WHITE HOUSE

Sasha is the youngest child to live in the White House since John F. Kennedy Jr. moved in as a baby in 1960. John-John, as he was affectionately called, was famously photographed as a toddler hiding under his daddy's desk in the Oval Office.

Having young children like Sasha and her sister in the White House helps Americans identify with Michelle and Barack, who share the same concerns as many other parents. In addition to bringing a sense of fun and a youthful vibe to the White House, Sasha and Malia are now **role models**, too. Gina Shropshire, a college professor who specializes in discussing what shapes the identities of African-American students, said,

❝These two children are, literally and figuratively, a new face for young black children.❞

Decorating Her Room

Sasha and her sister moved into one of the oldest and most distinguished homes in America, full of history and priceless antiques. But that didn't mean Sasha couldn't pick her own bedroom and decorate it exactly the way she wanted.

The first family spends most of its time on the second and third floors of the White House in private quarters that almost no one outside the family ever gets to see. Before she moved in, Sasha selected furniture for her room from photographs. She was also allowed to bring her own furniture. Sasha chose her room's color and what to hang on the walls. She was allowed to bring her Jonas Brothers posters to the White House.

PERKS OF PRESIDENTIAL KIDS

One of the sweetest things about being a kid in the White House is that entertainers and celebrities often visit—at their request. Sasha and Malia were issued an invitation to appear on one of

Barack and Michelle get Sasha and Malia ready for their first day of school at Sidwell Friends, January 5, 2009. Sasha was excited to meet her classmates at her new school and to move into the White House, where she had been allowed to decorate her own room.

their favorite television shows, *Hannah Montana*, before they even moved into the White House. A spokesman for the Disney channel said,

> **❝We're pleased that Malia and Sasha are fans, and as long as their parents say it's OK, they are invited to the set of *Hannah Montana* and all Disney shows, for a guest role or a visit.❞**

Teenager Miley Cyrus, who plays the title role in the show, also has a famous father, country singer Billy Ray Cyrus. Miley

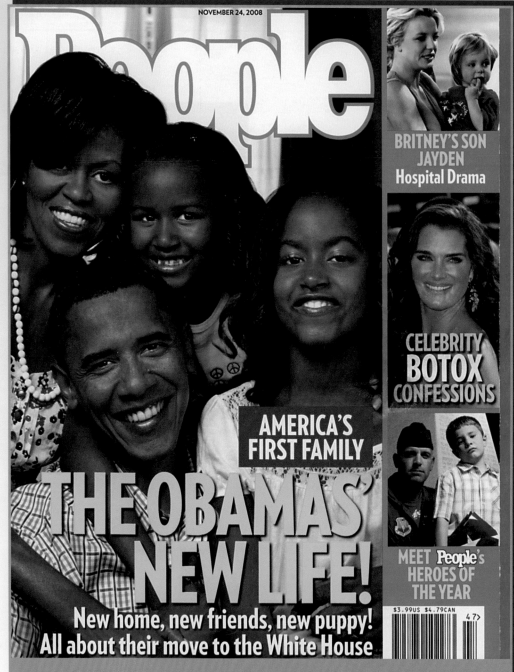

NOVEMBER 24, 2008

People

AMERICA'S FIRST FAMILY

THE OBAMAS' NEW LIFE!

New home, new friends, new puppy!
All about their move to the White House

BRITNEY'S SON JAYDEN
Hospital Drama

CELEBRITY BOTOX CONFESSIONS

MEET **People**'s HEROES OF THE YEAR

$3.99US $4.79CAN

47>

People magazine cover story, "The Obamas' New Life." One of the best parts of the family's life in the White House is that Barack is no longer on the road, so Sasha can see her dad every day and share what he calls "this great adventure."

said Sasha and Malia remind her of herself before she achieved fame in her own right. Back then she found herself making appearances on television simply because her father is a star.

HANGING WITH DAD

Perhaps the best gift of all for Sasha is not that she now spends time hanging out with celebrities. Instead, it is finally having the opportunity to hang with her father. As Michelle told a reporter for the television show *60 Minutes,*

> **❝I envision the kids coming home from school and being able to run across the way to the Oval Office and see their dad before they start their homework. And having breakfast. And he'll be there to tuck them in at night.❞**

A LETTER FROM DAD

For two years Sasha has traveled long distances and endured great absences during her father's presidential campaign. At this beginning of a new chapter for the first family, Barack wrote a letter to his daughters explaining why he took them on this journey, and what he wants for them—and for every child in America:

> **❝These are the things I want for you—to grow up in a world with no limits on your dreams and no achievements beyond your reach, and to grow into compassionate, committed women who will help build that world. And I want every child to have the same chances to learn and dream and grow and thrive that you girls have. That's why I've taken our family on this great adventure.**
>
> **I am so proud of both of you. I love you more than you can ever know. And I am grateful every day for your patience, poise, grace, and humor as we prepare to start our new life together in the White House.❞**

1961   Father, Barack Obama, is born in Hawaii on August 4.

1964   Mother, Michelle Robinson, is born in Chicago on January 17.

1992   Parents marry.

1996   Barack wins a seat in the Illinois State Senate.

1998   Sister, Malia, is born in Chicago on July 4.

2001   Natasha (Sasha) is born in Chicago on June 10.

2004   Barack delivers keynote address at Democratic National Convention.

Barack is elected to the U.S. Senate.

2007   Barack declares his candidacy for president of the United States.

2008   Barack elected 44th president of the United States.

2009   Sasha and Malia attend Sidwell Friends, a private school in Washington, D.C.

The family moves into the White House on January 20.

- Sasha eats mostly organic food grown without pesticides.

- Sasha's allowance is $1 a week.

- She is allowed to watch television for one hour a day.

- Sasha is responsible for walking her puppy and cleaning up after it.

- Sasha loves dancing and believes she might enjoy a career as a professional dancer.

- When Sasha's grandmother, Marian Robinson, babysits, she lets Sasha stay up late and watch lots of television.

- Everyone in Sasha's family has been given a code name by the Secret Service, the agency that protects them. Sasha is called Rosebud.

- The White House has its own movie theater, bowling alley, swimming pool, and tennis courts.

- The White House has a children's garden that is hidden from the public's view. In the garden are cement handprints from former White House kids Amy Carter, Chelsea Clinton, and Barbara and Jenna Bush.

caucus—Process used by some states to award delegates to presidential candidates; in a caucus, voters meet in groups and cast their ballots in public, often by a show of hands.

delegates—Officials of the Republican and Democratic parties selected through primaries and caucuses and designated to cast votes to nominate presidential candidates at the party conventions, based on the number of popular votes the candidates received in the spring contests.

gavel—Wooden mallet used to call an official meeting to order, usually by the chairman.

independents—Voters who are unaffiliated with the Democratic or Republican political parties.

keynote address—The major speech delivered at the opening of the national political conventions, or similar events, intended to set the tone for the conventions and inspire the delegates and others who attend.

motorcade—Long line of cars, often led and trailed by police vehicles, used to transport a head of state or other dignitary over city streets or highways.

pedigree—Traceable line of distinguished ancestors.

role models—Celebrities, athletes, and community members who serve as inspirations to ordinary people who want to be like them.

Books and Periodicals

Colbert, David. *Michelle Obama: Meet the First Lady*. New York: Harper Collins, 2009.

Fiore, Fay and Baum, Geraldine. "Malia and Sasha's Big Move," *Los Angeles Times* (November 18, 2008).

Kugler, Sara. "Obama and Family Hand Out Food at Chicago Church," *Associated Press* (November 26, 2008).

Marche, Stephen. "Daddy, What City Are You In?" *The Financial Post* (August 30, 2008).

Obama, Barack: *Dreams from My Father: A Story of Race and Inheritance*. New York: Crown Publishers, 2004.

Wead, Doug. *All the President's Children: Triumph and Tragedy in the Lives of America's First Families*. New York: Atria Books, 2004.

Web Sites

www.myspace.com/barackobama

Barack Obama's MySpace Page. Visitors can find a biography of Barack, click on "Meet the Obamas," watch video of Barack's speeches, and connect with Barack elsewhere on the Web such as YouTube, Facebook, and Twitter.

www.constitutioncenter.org

Students can find out more about the National Constitution Center in Philadelphia where Barack gave his speech on race. The site contains a section for students that offers fun facts about the Constitution and interactive games that test knowledge of voting rights and what kids might do if they had to make the decisions made by President Abraham Lincoln, the president Barack admires most.

http://www.huffingtonpost.com/2008/11/06/sasha-obama-see-how-shes_n_141678.html

Sasha Slide Show. Visitors can view photographs of the littlest Obama from 2004 through the present, compiled by the Web site Huffington Post.

www.sidwell.edu

Sidwell Friends. Web site for the private school in Washington, D.C., attended by Sasha. Students can learn about the school's history and what second graders like Sasha learn in the classroom.

page

ABOUT THE AUTHOR

Gail Snyder is a freelance writer and advertising copywriter who has written more than ten books for young readers. She lives in Chalfont, Pennsylvania, with her husband, Hal, and daughter Ashley.